D1325976

52 THINGS TO DO WHILE YOU POO
THE 1970s EDITION

AN HACHETTE UK COMPANY
WWW.HACHETTE.CO.UK

SUMMERSDALE PUBLISHERS LTD
PART OF OCTOPUS PUBLISHING GROUP LIMITED
CARMELITE HOUSE
50 VICTORIA EMBANKMENT
LONDON
EC4Y 0DZ
UK

WWW.SUMMERSDALE.COM
PRINTED AND BOUND IN CHINA
ISBN: 978-1-80007-432-3

SUBSTANTIAL DISCOUNTS ON BULK QUANTITIES OF SUMMERSDALE BOOKS
ARE AVAILABLE TO CORPORATIONS, PROFESSIONAL ASSOCIATIONS AND
OTHER ORGANIZATIONS. FOR DETAILS CONTACT GENERAL ENQUIRIES:
TELEPHONE: +44 (0) 1243 771107 OR EMAIL: ENQUIRIES@SUMMERSDALE.COM.

52 THINGS TO DO WHILE YOU POO

THE 1970s EDITION

HUGH JASSBURN

IF YOU GREW UP IN THE 1970s, YOU KNOW THAT NOTHING COMPARES TO THE MUSIC, FASHION, TOYS, TV, FILMS AND SHEER *FEEL* OF THAT DECADE. BUT HOW MUCH CAN YOU REALLY REMEMBER? WHEN YOU NEXT TAKE A TRIP TO THE TOILET, THIS COLOURFUL COLLECTION OF PUZZLES, ACTIVITIES AND TRIVIA WILL SERVE AS A LEISURELY STROLL DOWN MEMORY LANE, DUSTING OFF HALF-REMEMBERED FACTS AND EVEN FILLING IN A FEW GAPS.

THIS PAIR ONLY APPEARS ONCE
ON THE OPPOSITE PAGE

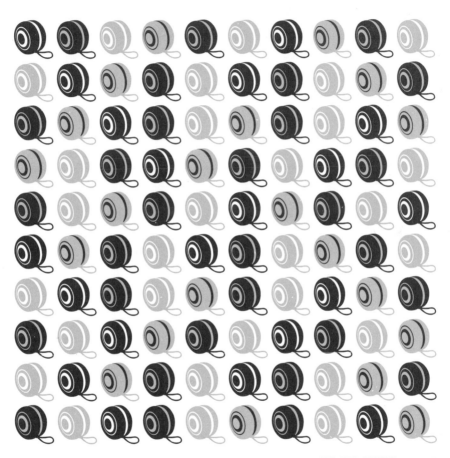

"ALOHA FROM HAWAII" WAS A CONCERT BROADCAST ON 14 JANUARY 1973 VIA SATELLITE TO INTERNATIONAL AUDIENCES. WHO WAS THE STAR?

A) ELTON JOHN

B) ELVIS

C) MARVIN GAYE

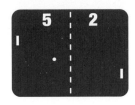

IN 1972, ATARI RELEASED THE ARCADE GAME
***PONG,* BUT THE EARLY MACHINES BROKE**
DOWN VERY QUICKLY. WHY?

A) TOO MUCH BEER WAS SPILLED ON THEM

**B) PLAYERS WERE SHAKING THEM
OUT OF FRUSTRATION**

**C) THEY WERE SO POPULAR THEY OVERFLOWED
WITH COINS AND STOPPED WORKING**

IT'S 14 JANUARY 1970 AND DIANA ROSS IS LEAVING THE SUPREMES...

52 THINGS TO DO WHILE YOU POO...

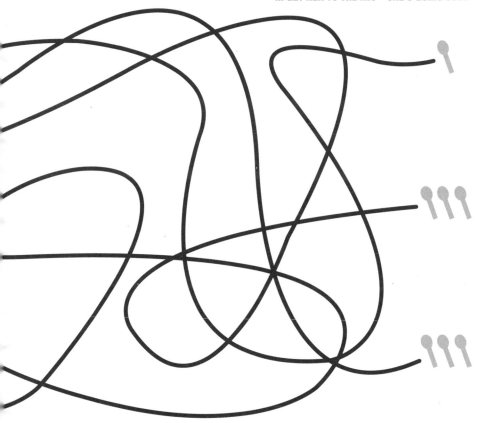

BRANDT (WILLIAM, CHANCELLOR, WEST GERMANY, 69–74)

WILSON (HAROLD, PRIME MINISTER, UNITED KINGDOM, 74–76)

FUKUDA (TAKEO, PRIME MINISTER, JAPAN, 76–78)

CARTER (JIMMY, PRESIDENT, USA, 77–81)

MEIR (GOLDA, PRIME MINISTER, ISRAEL, 69–74)

WHITLAM (GOUGH, PRIME MINISTER, AUSTRALIA, 72–75)

PARK (CHUNG-HEE, PRESIDENT, SOUTH KOREA, 63–79)

POMPIDOU (GEORGES, PRESIDENT, FRANCE, 69–74)

DESAI (MORARJI, PRIME MINISTER, INDIA, 77–79)

CLARK (JOE, PRIME MINISTER, CANADA, 79–80)

BHUTTO (ZULFIKAR ALI, PRESIDENT, PAKISTAN, 71–73)

R W T T N C E R U Y
E A S D O L M F O P
T M L K S A T J D A
R N B V L R D D I R
A K J T I K N E P K
C D I T W R A S M W
B H U T T O R A O E
W G F K D S B I P R
K J G H U R G H E A
M L P O I F U Y T M

MUSIC, AT ITS ESSENCE, IS WHAT GIVES US MEMORIES. AND THE LONGER A SONG HAS EXISTED IN OUR LIVES, THE MORE MEMORIES WE HAVE OF IT.

STEVIE WONDER

IT'S 28 SEPTEMBER 1976 – GET TO THE SHOP TO BUY STEVIE WONDER'S NEW ALBUM!

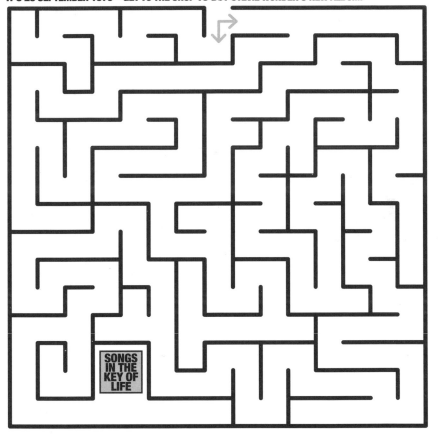

TIDY UP THE TUNE TIMELINE – MATCH THE SONG TO THE YEAR IT WAS RELEASED

SUPERSTITION

LET IT BE

WATERLOO

STAIRWAY TO HEAVEN

ANARCHY IN THE UK

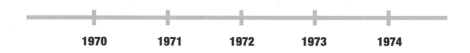

1970   1971   1972   1973   1974

DREAMS

MISS YOU

LONDON CALLING

GOODBYE YELLOW BRICK ROAD

BOHEMIAN RHAPSODY

1975   1976   1977   1978   1979

WHEN FILMING OF THE 1975 HIT *JAWS* BEGAN, THE ANIMATRONIC SHARKS KEPT BREAKING DOWN BECAUSE THEY HAD NEVER BEEN TESTED IN SALT WATER. WHAT NICKNAME DID DIRECTOR STEVEN SPIELBERG GIVE THEM?

A) GREAT WHITE TURDS

B) GREAT WHITE FLAWS

C) GREAT WHITE FLOPS

HOT PANTS

FLARES

PONCHO

PLATFORM SHOES

WHICH 1970s FASHION ICON DID THE DUO SONNY AND CHER MAKE FAMOUS?

EACH 2x2 BLOCK, COLUMN AND ROW SHOULD CONTAIN THE FOUR 1970s PARTY FAVOURITES

FONDUE

VOL-AU-VENT

QUICHE LORRAINE

SNOWBALL

THIS PAIR ONLY APPEARS ONCE
ON THE OPPOSITE PAGE

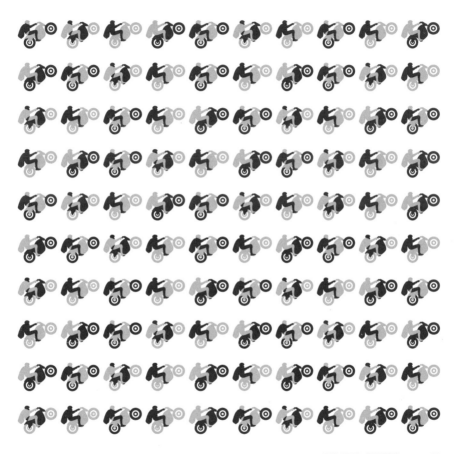

THE WORLD'S FIRST COMMERCIAL JUMBO JET FLIGHT TOOK PLACE ON 22 JANUARY 1970, CARRYING 332 PASSENGERS AND 18 CREW MEMBERS. WHAT WAS THE ROUTE?

A) NEW YORK TO PARIS

B) LONDON TO NEW YORK

C) NEW YORK TO LONDON

WHO INVENTED AND MADE THE FIRST COMMERCIALLY AVAILABLE FLOPPY DISK IN 1971?

A) IBM

B) ATARI

C) MICROSOFT

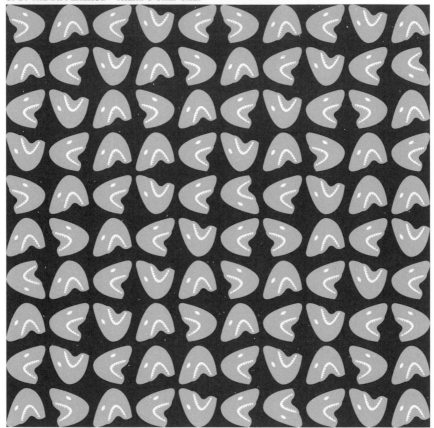

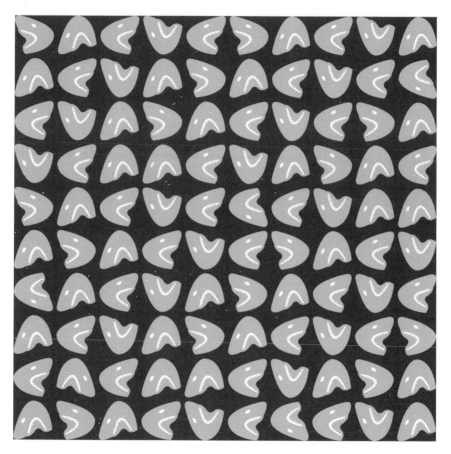

I WOULD RATHER WAKE UP
IN THE MIDDLE OF NOWHERE THAN
IN ANY CITY ON EARTH.

STEVE McQUEEN

IT'S 1970, SO GET STEVE TO HIS PORSCHE – HE NEEDS TO FILM *LE MANS*!

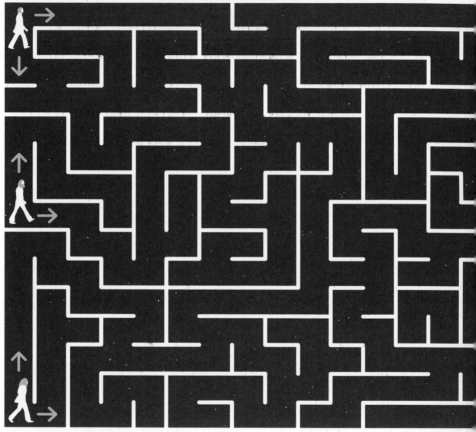

**ON 28 FEBRUARY 1971, EVEL KNIEVEL
SET A NEW WORLD RECORD WITH HIS
HARLEY-DAVIDSON XR-750 AT THE ONTARIO
MOTOR SPEEDWAY IN ONTARIO, CALIFORNIA.
HOW MANY CARS DID HE JUMP?**

A) 13

B) 19

C) 30

THE FIRST *MR MEN* BOOKS WERE PUBLISHED ON 10 AUGUST 1971, BUT WHO WAS THE FIRST CHARACTER THAT AUTHOR ROGER HARGREAVES CREATED?

A) MR TICKLE

B) MR STRONG

C) LITTLE MISS PRINCESS

DAMON (MATT, 8 OCTOBER 1970)

SPENCER (OCTAVIA, 25 MAY 1970)

MARTIN (CHRIS, 2 MARCH 1977)

RYDER (WINONA, 29 OCTOBER 1971)

REYNOLDS (RYAN, 23 OCTOBER 1976)

ELBA (IDRIS, 6 SEPTEMBER 1972)

DiCAPRIO (LEONARDO, 11 NOVEMBER 1974)

BECKINSALE (KATE, 26 JULY 1973)

MIJU OH (SANDRA, 20 JULY 1971)

KARDASHIAN (KOURTNEY, 18 APRIL 1979)

```
N E D L O X H M N N
R L I V E R C V A B
E A D I C A P R I O
C S W E R T Y Y H N
N N Y U I O P D S I
E I W E A N Y E A T
P K A B R T O R D R
S C L S D F G M R A
R E Y N O L D S A M
I B M I J U O H K D
```

YOU'RE OFF TO A DISCO – FIND YOUR FLARES!

EACH 2x2 BLOCK, COLUMN AND ROW SHOULD CONTAIN THE FOUR OBJECTS

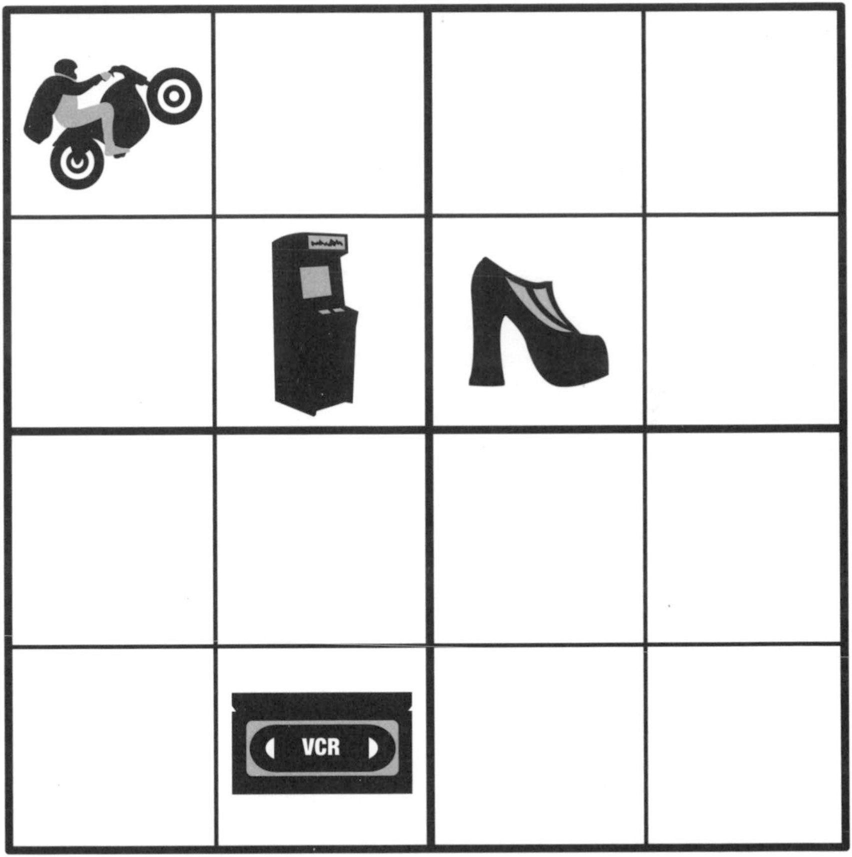
VCR

WE'RE HERE TO PUT A DENT IN THE UNIVERSE. OTHERWISE WHY ELSE EVEN BE HERE?

STEVE JOBS

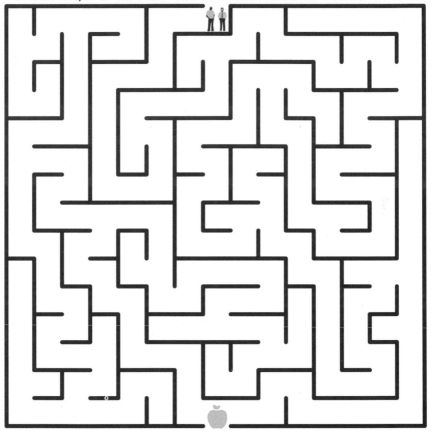

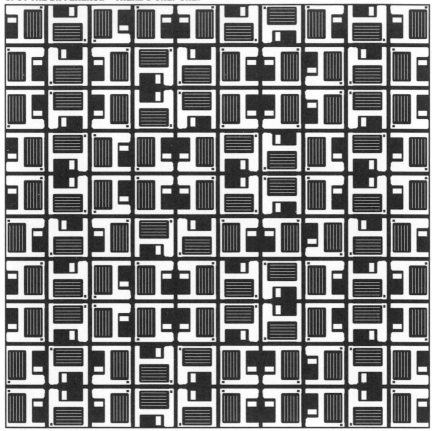

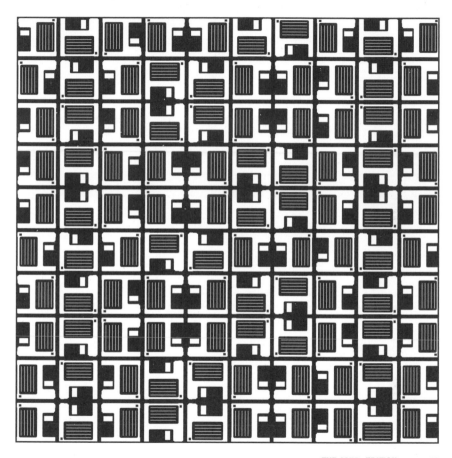

THIS PAIR ONLY APPEARS ONCE
ON THE OPPOSITE PAGE

ON 20 SEPTEMBER 1973, FORMER NO. 1 TENNIS PLAYER BOBBY RIGGS PLAYED IN "THE BATTLE OF THE SEXES" AFTER SAYING NO WOMAN COULD BEAT HIM. WHO WON 6-4, 6-3, 6-3?

A) BILLIE JEAN KING

B) BOBBY RIGGS

C) CHRIS EVERT

WHO IS CREDITED WITH INVENTING THE FIRST AFFORDABLE POCKET-SIZED CALCULATOR IN THE EARLY 1970s?

A) BILL GATES

B) CLIVE SINCLAIR

C) STEVE WOZNIAK

BRING THE
YO-YO TO LIFE
(USING 1970s COLOURS)

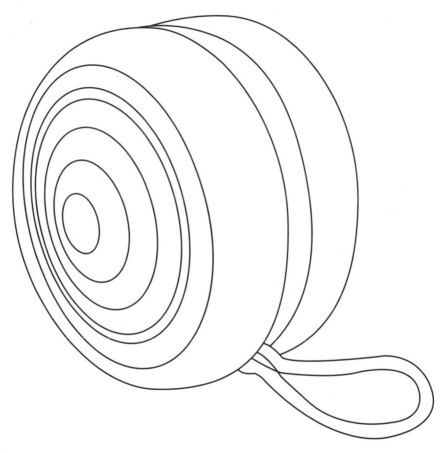

ON 21 JANUARY 1976, THE FIRST
COMMERCIAL CONCORDE FLIGHT TOOK
PLACE FROM LONDON TO PARIS.
**FIND THE CONCORDE, GET ON IT
AND MAKE HISTORY!**

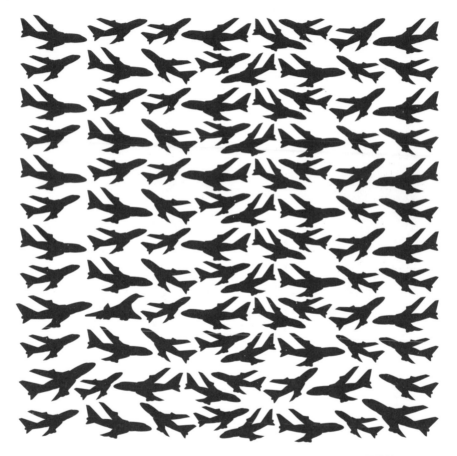

GLAM REALLY DID PLANT SEEDS FOR A NEW IDENTITY. I THINK A LOT OF KIDS NEEDED THAT – THAT SENSE OF REINVENTION.

DAVID BOWIE

IT'S 3 JULY 1973, SO GET BOWIE TO THE STAGE FOR HIS FINAL PERFORMANCE AS ZIGGY STARDUST!

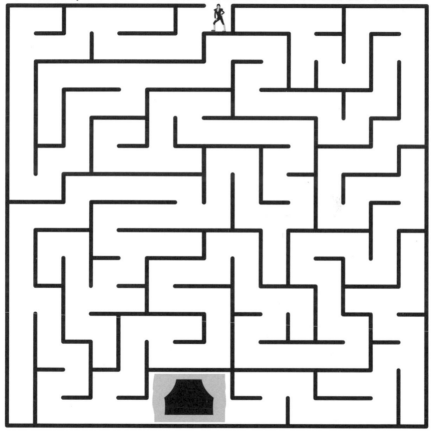

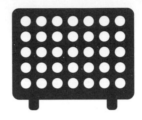

WHAT DOES THE OFFICIAL CONNECT FOUR RACK CONSIST OF?

A) 6 ROWS AND 7 COLUMNS

B) 7 ROWS AND 8 COLUMNS

C) 6 ROWS AND 8 COLUMNS

THE WORD "FONDUE" COMES FROM THE FRENCH VERB *FONDRE*. WHAT IS THE ENGLISH TRANSLATION?

A) TO DIP

B) TO MELT

C) TO MOP

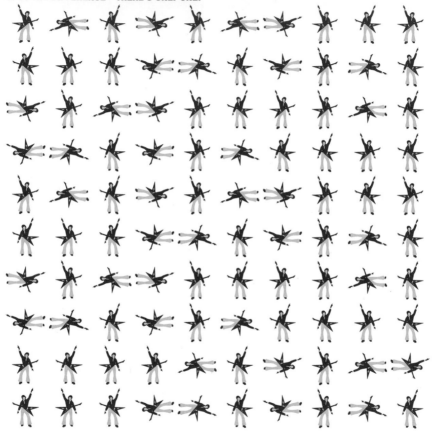

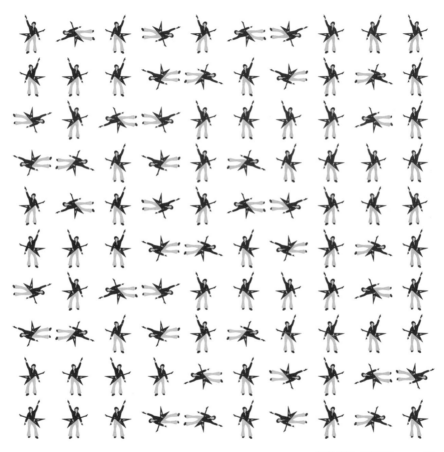

THIS PAIR ONLY APPEARS ONCE
ON THE OPPOSITE PAGE

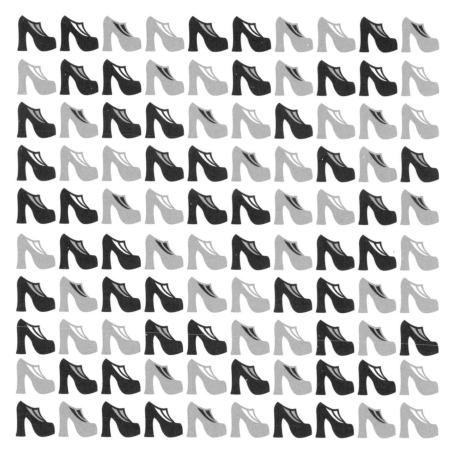

TRAVOLTA (JOHN)

NEWTON-JOHN (OLIVIA)

DUNAWAY (FAYE)

STREISAND (BARBRA)

REDFORD (ROBERT)

REYNOLDS (BURT)

FAWCETT (FARRAH)

OSMOND (DONNY AND MARIE)

PRYOR (RICHARD)

WILDER (GENE)

A	S	D	F	O	S	M	O	N	D
G	W	P	R	Y	O	R	P	H	I
T	R	A	V	O	L	T	A	O	O
T	E	E	K	L	G	P	R	J	Y
E	Y	J	D	A	H	E	G	N	A
C	N	S	M	F	D	D	F	O	W
W	O	A	C	L	O	V	B	T	A
A	L	N	I	M	X	R	L	W	N
F	D	W	O	I	U	T	D	E	U
I	S	T	R	E	I	S	A	N	D

YOU RECORDED AN EPISODE OF YOUR FAVOURITE SHOW – FIND THE VIDEO TAPE WITH *M*A*S*H* ON IT!

1970s

**IN APRIL 1974, ABBA SHOT TO WORLDWIDE
FAME AT THE BRIGHTON DOME IN ENGLAND
WITH WHICH ONE OF THEIR HIT SONGS?**

A) "DANCING QUEEN"

B) "MAMMA MIA"

C) "WATERLOO"

"THE RUMBLE IN THE JUNGLE" WAS A BOXING MATCH THAT TOOK PLACE ON 30 OCTOBER 1974 BETWEEN WHICH TWO HEAVYWEIGHT BOXERS?

A) GEORGE FOREMAN AND MUHAMMAD ALI

B) MUHAMMAD ALI AND JOE FRAZIER

C) JOE FRAZIER AND GEORGE FOREMAN

EACH 2x2 BLOCK, COLUMN AND ROW SHOULD CONTAIN THE FOUR 1970s HAIRSTYLES

THE SHAG

DREADLOCKS

THE PAGEBOY

THE MULLET

YOU'VE KICKED YOUR BEANBAG INTO NEXT DOOR'S VEGETABLE PATCH! FIND IT!

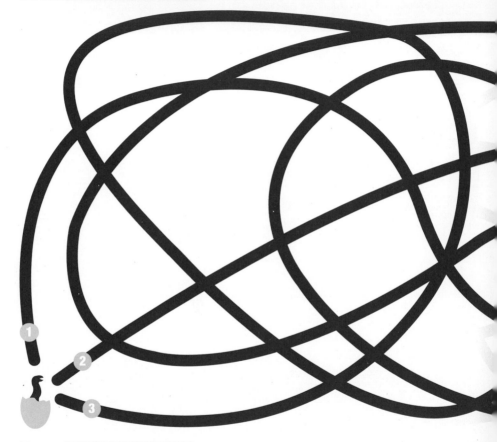

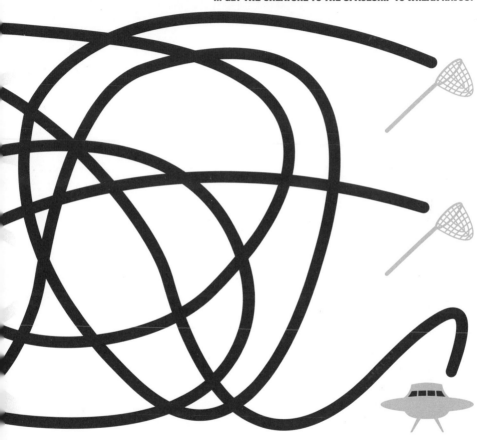

MY BIGGEST MISTAKE
WAS MY BEST LESSON...
YOU DON'T LEARN ANYTHING
WHEN EVERYTHING IS
GOING PERFECTLY.

OLIVIA NEWTON-JOHN

IT'S 1978 AND GREASE IS THE WORD! GET DANNY TO SANDY!

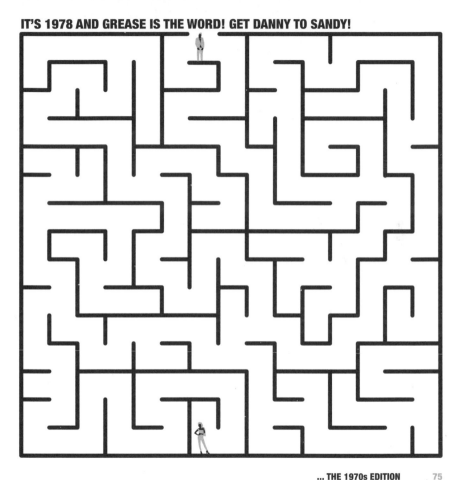

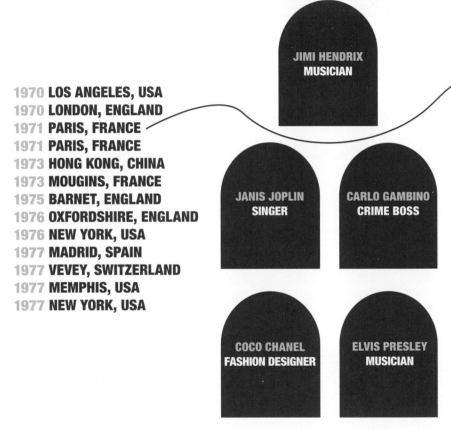

1970 **LOS ANGELES, USA**
1970 **LONDON, ENGLAND**
1971 **PARIS, FRANCE**
1971 **PARIS, FRANCE**
1973 **HONG KONG, CHINA**
1973 **MOUGINS, FRANCE**
1975 **BARNET, ENGLAND**
1976 **OXFORDSHIRE, ENGLAND**
1976 **NEW YORK, USA**
1977 **MADRID, SPAIN**
1977 **VEVEY, SWITZERLAND**
1977 **MEMPHIS, USA**
1977 **NEW YORK, USA**

JIMI HENDRIX
MUSICIAN

JANIS JOPLIN
SINGER

CARLO GAMBINO
CRIME BOSS

COCO CHANEL
FASHION DESIGNER

ELVIS PRESLEY
MUSICIAN

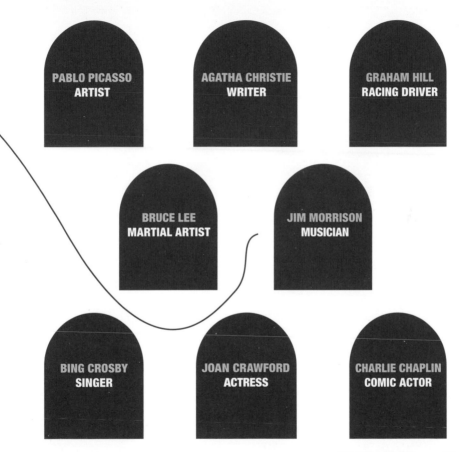

PABLO PICASSO
ARTIST

AGATHA CHRISTIE
WRITER

GRAHAM HILL
RACING DRIVER

BRUCE LEE
MARTIAL ARTIST

JIM MORRISON
MUSICIAN

BING CROSBY
SINGER

JOAN CRAWFORD
ACTRESS

CHARLIE CHAPLIN
COMIC ACTOR

WHAT MIDDLE NAME DID REGINALD DWIGHT CHOOSE WHEN HE CHANGED HIS NAME TO ELTON JOHN ON 7 JANUARY 1972?

A) APHRODITE

B) ZEUS

C) HERCULES

IN 1973, THE ENGINEER MARTIN COOPER INVENTED THE HANDHELD CELLULAR MOBILE PHONE. WHAT COMPANY DID HE WORK FOR?

A) BELL

B) MOTOROLA

C) SONY

THIS PAIR ONLY APPEARS ONCE
ON THE OPPOSITE PAGE

SUMMER (DONNA)

JOHN (ELTON)

KINKS (THE)

ZEPPELIN (LED)

WONDER (STEVIE)

ABBA

BOWIE (DAVID)

EAGLES (THE)

SKYNYRD (LYNYRD)

SIMON (CARLY)

R	S	K	Y	N	Y	R	D	K	L
E	N	W	K	G	I	N	K	I	N
M	I	O	F	P	D	A	S	N	O
M	L	N	G	R	H	J	K	K	M
U	E	D	E	A	G	L	E	S	I
S	P	E	X	I	S	A	Z	N	S
W	P	R	E	T	W	R	H	T	A
L	E	P	O	D	I	O	U	B	Y
K	Z	J	H	G	J	F	B	D	S
G	U	R	W	F	L	A	K	B	A

THE CHARACTERS IN WHICH POPULAR 1970s ARCADE GAME WERE MODELLED ON OCTOPUSES, SQUIDS AND CRABS?

A) *BREAKOUT*

B) *SPACE INVADERS*

C) *PAC-MAN*

QUEEN
GREATEST HITS

THE BAND QUEEN'S LOGO WAS CREATED AND ILLUSTRATED BY FREDDIE MERCURY – WHAT INSPIRED THE INDIVIDUAL ELEMENTS?

A) THE STAR SIGNS OF THE BAND MEMBERS

B) THE BAND'S FAVOURITE ANIMALS

C) THE STATUES OF BUCKINGHAM PALACE

WELCOME TO THE ANAGRAM MOVIE THEATRE – CAN YOU WORK OUT WHAT FILM IS SHOWING?

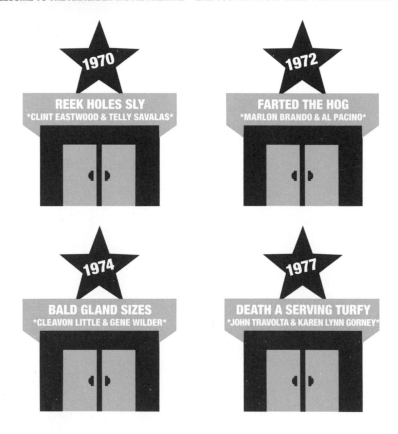

1970
REEK HOLES SLY
CLINT EASTWOOD & TELLY SAVALAS

1972
FARTED THE HOG
MARLON BRANDO & AL PACINO

1974
BALD GLAND SIZES
CLEAVON LITTLE & GENE WILDER

1977
DEATH A SERVING TURFY
JOHN TRAVOLTA & KAREN LYNN GORNEY

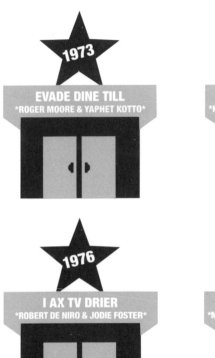

★ 1973 ★

EVADE DINE TILL
ROGER MOORE & YAPHET KOTTO

★ 1975 ★

OVERFEED WITH PSST
KATHARINE ROSS & PAULA PRENTISS

★ 1976 ★

I AX TV DRIER
ROBERT DE NIRO & JODIE FOSTER

★ 1971 ★

COCOA RANK LEGWORK
MALCOLM MCDOWELL & PATRICK MAGEE

FIND 1970

1 7 9 0 1 0 9 7 1 7 0 7 1 9 7 9 1 7 0 7
7 1 7 9 0 1 0 9 7 1 7 0 7 1 9 7 9 1 7 0
0 7 1 9 7 9 1 7 0 7 1 7 9 0 1 0 9 7 1 7
7 0 7 1 7 9 0 1 0 9 7 1 7 0 7 1 0 7 9 1
7 1 9 7 0 1 0 9 7 1 7 0 7 1 9 7 9 1 7 0
1 7 9 0 1 0 9 7 1 7 0 7 1 9 7 9 1 7 0 7
7 0 7 1 7 9 0 1 0 9 7 1 7 0 7 1 9 7 9 1
1 7 0 7 1 7 9 0 1 0 9 7 1 7 0 7 1 9 7 9
7 9 0 1 0 9 7 1 7 0 7 1 9 7 9 1 7 0 7 1
1 7 9 0 1 0 9 7 1 7 0 7 1 9 7 9 1 7 0 7
7 1 9 7 9 1 7 0 7 1 7 9 0 1 0 9 7 1 7 0
0 7 1 7 9 0 1 0 9 7 1 7 0 7 1 9 7 9 1 7
1 7 9 0 1 0 9 7 1 7 0 7 1 9 7 9 1 7 0 7
7 9 0 1 0 9 7 1 7 0 7 1 9 7 9 1 7 0 7 1
0 7 1 7 9 0 1 0 9 7 1 7 0 7 1 9 7 9 1 7
7 0 7 1 7 9 0 1 0 9 7 1 7 0 7 1 9 7 9 1
7 9 0 1 9 1 0 1 7 0 7 1 9 7 9 1 7 0 7 1
9 0 1 0 9 7 1 7 0 7 1 9 7 9 1 7 0 7 1 7
7 1 7 9 0 1 0 9 7 1 7 0 7 1 9 7 9 1 7 0
0 7 1 7 9 0 1 0 9 7 1 7 0 7 1 9 7 9 1 7

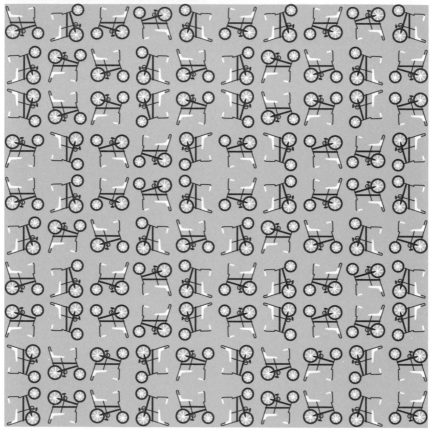

52 THINGS TO DO WHILE YOU POO...

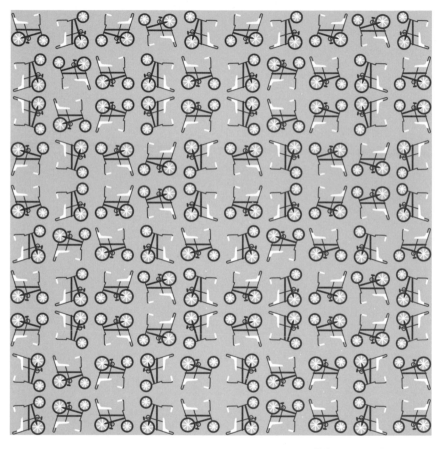

IN 1979, WHICH ATHLETE BROKE THREE WORLD RECORDS IN 41 DAYS?

A) SEBASTIAN COE

B) WILLIE DAVENPORT

C) TATYANA KAZANKINA

WHICH CAR BECAME THE MOST PRODUCED AUTOMOBILE IN THE WORLD IN 1972?

A) FORD MODEL T

B) CHEVROLET MONTE CARLO

C) VOLKSWAGEN BEETLE

EACH 2x2 BLOCK, COLUMN AND ROW SHOULD CONTAIN THE FOUR 1970s TOYS

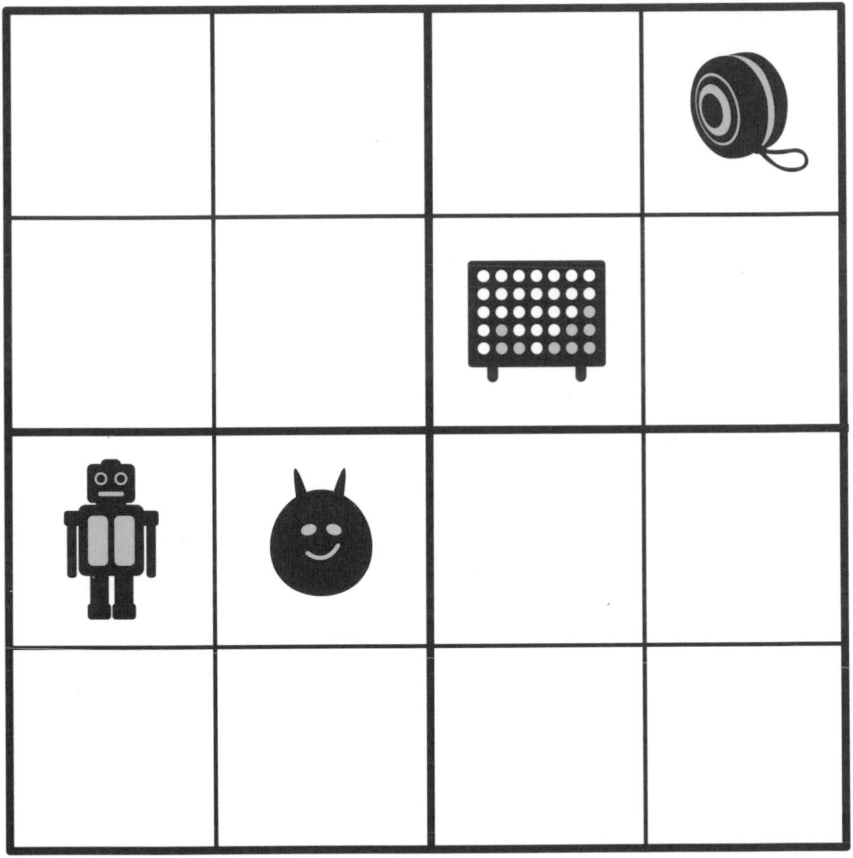

ON 1 JULY 1979, WHAT NEW DEVICE DID SONY START SELLING?

A) FM HEADPHONES

B) THE LONG-PLAY VIDEO CASSETTE RECORDER

C) THE SONY WALKMAN

WHICH BAND'S SELF-TITLED 1970 ALBUM IS CONSIDERED TO BE THE FIRST TRUE HEAVY METAL RECORD?

A) LED ZEPPELIN

B) BLACK SABBATH

C) DEEP PURPLE

IT'S ANAGRAM TV FROM THE 1970s – CAN YOU WORK OUT THE TV SHOW?

RASCALS
HEELING

A ANALYST
FINDS

UH A PREHENSILE
TOILET RIOT

HACK SHUTS
& TRY

A HA
VIEW O IF I

52 THINGS TO DO WHILE YOU POO...

ANSWERS

P6–7

P12–13

P8 B) ELVIS
P9 C) THEY WERE SO POPULAR THEY OVERFLOWED WITH COINS AND STOPPED WORKING
P10–11

P15

P18 **A) GREAT WHITE TURDS**
P19 **FLARES**
P20–21

P16–17

P22–23

P29

P24 **C) NEW YORK TO LONDON**
P25 **A) IBM**
P26–27

52 THINGS TO DO WHILE YOU POO...

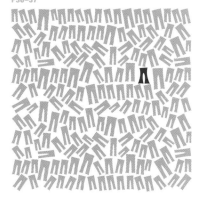

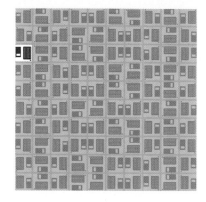

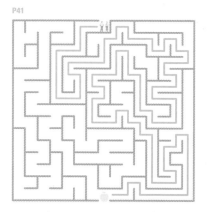

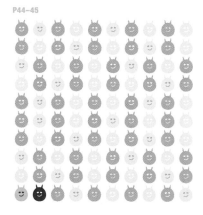

52 THINGS TO DO WHILE YOU POO...

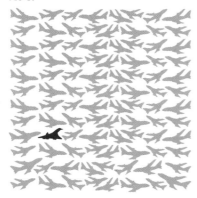

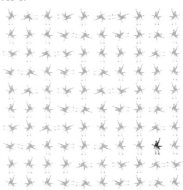

P60–61

P62–63

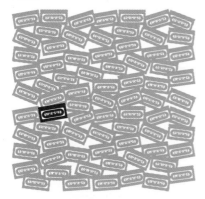

52 THINGS TO DO WHILE YOU POO...

P64–65

P66 **C) "WATERLOO"**
P67 **A) FOREMAN AND ALI**
P68–69

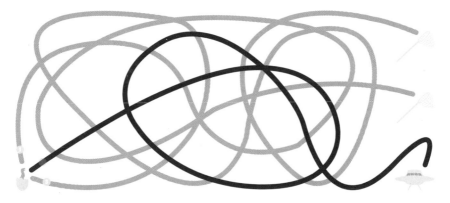

JIMI HENDRIX 1970 LONDON ENGLAND	PABLO PICASSO 1973 MOUGINS FRANCE	AGATHA CHRISTIE 1976 OXFORDSHIRE ENGLAND	GRAHAM HILL 1975 BARNET ENGLAND
JANIS JOPLIN 1970 LOS ANGELES USA	CARLO GAMBINO 1976 NEW YORK USA	BRUCE LEE 1973 HONG KONG CHINA	JIM MORRISON 1971 PARIS FRANCE
COCO CHANEL 1971 PARIS FRANCE	ELVIS PRESLEY 1977 MEMPHIS TENNESSEE, USA	BING CROSBY 1977 MADRID SPAIN	JOAN CRAWFORD 1977 NEW YORK USA	CHARLIE CHAPLIN 1977 VEVEY SWITZERLAND

P78 C) HERCULES
P79 B) MOTOROLA
P80–81

P82–83

52 THINGS TO DO WHILE YOU POO...

1970 KELLY'S HEROES

1972 THE GODFATHER

1974 BLAZING SADDLES

1977 SATURDAY NIGHT FEVER

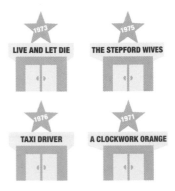

1973 LIVE AND LET DIE

1975 THE STEPFORD WIVES

1976 TAXI DRIVER

1971 A CLOCKWORK ORANGE

```
1 7 9 0 1 0 9 7 1 7 0 7 1 9 7 9 1 7 0 7
7 1 7 9 0 1 0 9 7 1 7 0 7 1 9 7 9 1 7 0
0 7 1 9 7 9 1 7 0 7 1 7 9 0 1 0 9 7 1 7
7 0 7 1 7 9 0 1 0 9 7 1 7 0 7 1 0 7 9 1
7 1 9 7 0 1 0 9 7 1 7 0 7 1 9 7 9 1 7 0
1 7 9 0 1 0 9 7 1 7 0 7 1 9 7 9 1 7 0 7
7 0 7 1 7 9 0 1 0 9 7 1 7 0 7 1 9 7 9 1
1 7 0 7 1 7 9 0 1 0 9 7 1 7 0 7 1 9 7 9
7 9 0 1 0 9 7 1 7 0 7 1 9 7 9 1 7 0 7 1
1 7 9 0 1 0 9 7 1 7 0 7 1 9 7 9 1 7 0 7
7 1 9 7 9 1 7 0 7 1 7 9 0 1 0 9 7 1 7 0
0 7 1 7 9 0 1 0 9 7 1 7 0 7 1 9 7 9 1 7
1 7 9 0 1 0 9 7 1 7 0 7 1 9 7 9 1 7 0 7
7 9 0 1 0 9 7 1 7 0 7 1 9 7 9 1 7 0 7 1
0 7 1 7 9 0 1 0 9 7 1 7 0 7 1 9 7 9 1 7
7 0 7 1 7 9 0 1 0 9 7 1 7 0 7 1 9 7 9 1
7 9 0 1 9 1 0 1 7 0 7 1 9 7 9 1 7 0 7 1
9 0 1 0 9 7 1 7 0 7 1 9 7 9 1 7 0 7 1 7
7 1 7 9 0 1 0 9 7 1 7 0 7 1 9 7 9 1 7 0
0 7 1 7 9 0 1 0 9 7 1 7 0 7 1 9 7 9 1 7
```

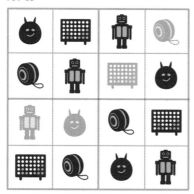

HAVE YOU ENJOYED THIS BOOK? IF SO, FIND US ON FACEBOOK AT SUMMERSDALE PUBLISHERS, ON TWITTER AT @SUMMERSDALE AND ON INSTAGRAM AT @SUMMERSDALEBOOKS AND GET IN TOUCH. WE'D LOVE TO HEAR FROM YOU!

WWW.SUMMERSDALE.COM